DECORATE

Your T-Shirts & Sweats

Contributing Writer: Susan Figliulo
Wearable Art Designers: Kristy Deutch, Hilary Elsinger

PUBLICATIONS
INTERNATIONAL, LTD.

ISBN: 1-56173-072-6

Pictured on front cover, clockwise from top left: Galaxy *(see page 19)*, Crayon Mania *(see page 25)*, Victorian Bouquet *(see page 41)*, and Holiday Packages *(see page 38)*.

Pictured on back cover: Impressionist Garden *(see page 56)*.

Wearable art designers: Kristy Deutch, Hilary Elsinger
"Veronica" designer: Dorothy Egan
Photography: Sam Griffith Studios

Contents

Introduction

They're funky and fabulous, sleek and sophisticated, romantic and fanciful, chic and classic. They're the most versatile item of clothing since civilization progressed beyond basic skins— and they seem to cry out for a personal statement as decoration.

What could we mean but the T-shirt? It's hard to remember when this ubiquitous garment existed only in white and was meant strictly to protect a man's real clothing—his shirt. Today, T-shirts—along with their cold-weather counterparts, sweatshirts—are the closest thing to a uniform for people of all ages. Babies everywhere wear little cotton shirts that tell the world "Grandma loves me," while older kids cover their chests (and often their backs) with announcements of their preferences in cartoon characters, rock groups, sports teams, or school activities. Even adults have come to consider these garments as sort of wearable bumper stickers.

And now we can use T-shirts and sweatshirts for another sort of personal expression: the visual creations that have come to be known as "wearable art." You can make your shirts express your personality by decorating them yourself. Creating wearable art is easy! You don't need to be a professional to create the designs in this book. No matter how intricate they appear, every one of the 17 designs has been created for the absolute beginner. No previous experience or knowledge is assumed.

The first few chapters will tell you just what you'll need and what you'll learn. In addition, each project lists every bit of equipment our designers used— brand names included!—so you can work with precisely what you'll need. Complete step-by-step instructions, each step illustrated with a photograph, make each project easy to understand and easy to do. And every project includes its own tips to make your way easier, plus variations to help you become your own designer.

So take a moment to browse through *Decorate Your T-Shirts and Sweats.* Look at the step-by-step instructions and notice how clearly you're able to "see" them. Think about what wonderful gifts these projects will make— especially when you announce that you made them yourself.

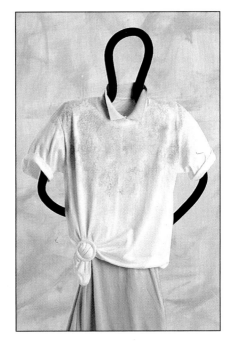

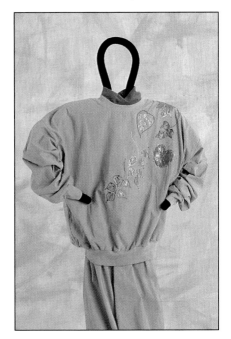

What You'll Learn

The techniques used in this book are easy to learn and just as easy to practice. You'll be surprised to see how various ways of applying paint can give your work a subtle and complex look. And you'll be even more surprised at how easy it is to combine two or more techniques to complement or accent each other.

When we say "technique," we mean doing something as simple as gluing objects onto a garment or squirting paint straight from a bottle onto fabric. We'll show you how to use brushes and other tools, including some common household items, to achieve the many different looks in this book. Several other easy techniques— appliqué without sewing, for example—are also explained and illustrated here.

There's no trick to mastering the techniques we use. Once you choose a project and actually follow it through our illustrated, step-by-step instructions, you'll see how easy it is to execute what may look like a very complicated piece of work. The techniques defined here are all used in creating the beautiful shirts in this book.

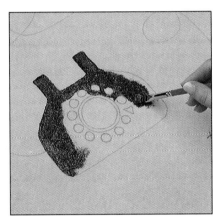

BASIC PAINTING: Using a brush or other tool to apply paint or dye directly to a fabric surface. In our "What You'll Need" section, you will see the variety of brushes and other applicators available. Each of the projects in this book tells you exactly which paints and tools we used, so you can simply duplicate our equipment when working on that project. As you become more accomplished, you'll be able to vary your choice of brushes to achieve different effects.

TEXTURE PAINTING: Applying paint or dye to fabric to achieve a three-dimensional effect that is slightly raised from the fabric itself. Many of the paints used in this book are called dimensional paints; they are designed to give this three-dimensional effect. Some texture painting is done simply by applying paint directly from its tube onto the fabric, then letting it dry into a raised line or shape. Texture painting can also be done with a paint containing an embellishing element such as glitter, small crystals, or tiny shreds of foil. When these paints dry, their three-dimensional effect is enhanced by those elements.

PRINTING WITH PAINT: Applying paint or dye to fabric using a stamp or other tool that has its own design. Commonly used tools include sponges and many elements from nature, such as leaves, fruits, and vegetables. (Think of the potato-stamping technique children learn: cutting a simple design from a potato, then dipping the carved end into paint to stamp on paper in a repeating pattern.)

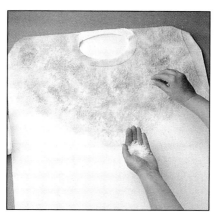

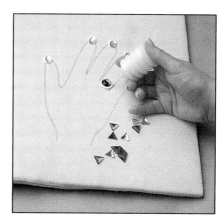

STENCILING WITH PAINT:
Applying paint or dye to fabric using a precut stencil. A precut stencil is a thin, flexible piece of plastic that can be used over and over again. Commercially made precut stencils can be purchased at craft stores, home decorating centers, art supply shops, and variety stores. To make your own stencil, simply cut the desired shape from a sheet of thin, flexible plastic, cardboard, or transparent adhesive-backed paper (such as Contact paper).

SALTING: Applying dye to dampened fabric, usually with a brush, and then covering the wet dye with salt. The salt is then left to dry. As the salt draws out moisture, it leaves a uniquely patterned effect suggesting motion. The salt is simply brushed off the fabric after drying.

GLUING: Attaching embellishments to fabric using fabric glue or dimensional paint. Fabric glue is specially formulated to withstand washing and must be used when the projects in this book call for it.

TRANSFERRING PATTERNS:
Transferring to fabric an image that is to be painted or embellished. To transfer a pattern, photocopy it or trace it from this book onto tracing paper (a transparent but sturdy tissuelike paper). Using a permanent ink, draw over the pattern, then retrace the lines with a pastel pencil or

tailor's chalk. Tape or pin the pattern, pencil side down, exactly where you want it on the fabric. Gently rub your fingertip along the pattern lines to transfer the pencil image onto the fabric. Before removing the pattern from the shirt, turn back a corner of the pattern and check to see that the image has been transferred.

Gently blow off excess pencil dust, then use a permanent marker to retrace the pattern lines on the fabric. Remove the remaining pencil image by tapping the pattern lines, causing the pencil dust to disperse. If your fabric is light enough, you may be able to slide the pattern under the shirt and trace directly onto the fabric.

NO-SEW APPLIQUÉ: Attaching fabric to fabric using a medium that causes them to adhere, such as dimensional paint, fabric glue, or adhesive web. Adhesive web allows you to simply iron the fabric in place on the shirt.

What You'll Need

Like the projects themselves, the paints, brushes, and other equipment you'll use to create the projects in this book are intended for beginners. All the tools and supplies you'll read about in these pages have been chosen because they're easy to handle and easy to master and because they get the job done. And they're widely available through many different sources, including craft shops, art supply stores, and variety stores.

The items you'll need for nearly every project we show are a shirt board (to hold your garment while you're working on it); masking tape (for attaching your shirt to the shirt board); a cup of water (for rinsing your brush or applicator); waxed paper or palette paper (for working with paint on a brush), and paper towels.

Even though a few of the projects you'll see in this book don't even require paint, a tube of paint remains the most fundamental piece of equipment for the wearable art we've created. Many varieties of paint are available; each project lists exactly what we used in working on that shirt.

PAINTS: Almost any acrylic paint can be adapted to use on fabric. And acrylics are nontoxic, so you needn't worry about using them in the home. The projects in this book call for either artist's

USING A SHIRT BOARD: When you're ready to paint a T-shirt or sweatshirt, you'll need to keep the surface taut and flat. The easiest way to do this is to affix the garment to a shirt board, which is a specially sized, wax-covered board that's described in "What You'll Need."

To use your shirt board, simply slide the board in between the front and back of the garment you're about to paint. Make sure the waxed side of the board is directly under the surface you want to paint. Pull the arms of the garment snugly behind the board, being careful not to stretch the fabric so tight that the garment's shape is changed. Use masking tape to fasten the arms onto the back of the board. Then pull the bottom of the shirt up behind the board and fasten it in the same way. Don't worry if the back isn't perfectly neat; your goal is to get a tight, flat fabric surface without stretching the garment out of shape.

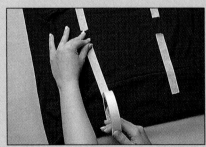

Often, we suggest bringing a design onto the sleeves, neckline, shoulders, or back of a shirt. Some projects even suggest decorating matching pants to create a coordinated outfit. To accomplish these variations, you'll need a board that accommodates a different shape. We tell you how to make your own board, in just the dimensions you want, in "What You'll Need." When you've made the board you want, simply affix the garment to it as described previously.

acrylics, acrylic dyes, dimensional paints, or embellished paints. Only dimensional and embellished paints, which are formulated for use on fabric, can be used directly from the tube. Artist's acrylics and some acrylic dyes must be thinned with a special mixture called textile medium and applied with brushes or other tools. With a few exceptions, these thinned paints also must be heat-set—that is, ironed or placed briefly in the dryer after being applied to fabric.

Dimensional paints are made by several companies, including Delta/Shiva, Tulip, and Galacraft. Basic dimensional paints include Galacraft Plain, Tulip Slick, and Delta Shiny Stuff for Fabric. Tulip Iridescent Fabric Paint, Delta Shiny Opalescent Fabric Paint, and Gala Color Pearl all give color in a pearlized finish. Glitter fabric paint becomes clear when it dries so all you see is the color of the glitter. Tulip Glitter Pen, Delta Glitter Stuff for Fabric, and Gala Color Glitter come in many colors. If you want an assortment of paints, you can try Tulip Fine Line Paint Writer. These are smaller tubes of paints that come in sets of several different colors.

Tulip Fashion Tints, available in jars, hold very fine glitter in a translucent, tinted medium. Tulip also makes Jumpin' Jeans Denim Paint, which offers neons and regular colors in a paint that's made for use on dark fabrics.

For a more fancy look, Crystal Gala Color and Tulip Candi Crystals contain coarse pieces of glitter that give a special sparkle. You can also try another fashion look by using Tulip Fiber Fun! and Galacraft Galafetti, which contain tiny pieces of shredded foil in a clear or tinted medium.

Delta and Grumbacher Dye are among the widely available acrylic dyes you may want to use in decorating garments. When you use artist's acrylics, you'll need

You can find a selection of fabric paints in many different colors and finishes.

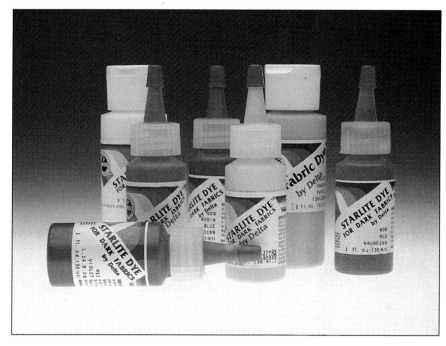

Dyes made specially for use on fabrics are available in a variety of colors.

a textile medium, which is a milky liquid that adapts these acrylics to fabric and helps them adhere. Usually it is spread on the fabric, with color applied on top of the medium. It's important to work rapidly when using textile medium because it dries quickly. For specific instructions, follow the directions on the bottle. When used with artist's acrylics, textile medium will leave a matte finish.

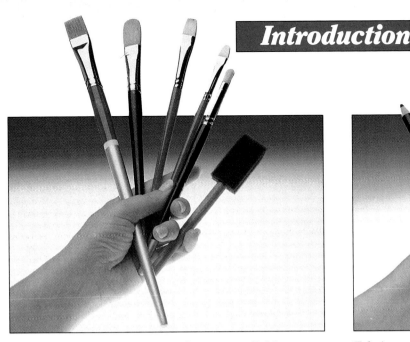

Many different shapes of brushes are available.

Fabric pens can be either permanent or "disappearing."

BRUSHES: With a selection almost as large as that of paint, shopping for brushes can be confusing! We'll tell you exactly which brush or applicator we used for each project in this book, but you may want to know a little about what you'll see when you look for equipment.

The brushes used in decorating clothing can be sponge brushes or bristle brushes. The sponge brush is a rectangle of fine-grain synthetic sponge cut to an angle at its tip and slit at the bottom to fit onto a wooden stick. Sponge brushes are available in several sizes—for simplicity's sake, we always use a 1-inch brush, but you can substitute. They're easy to care for by simply washing paint from them after using.

Bristle brushes come in a wide variety of sizes, widths, and degrees of fineness in their bristles. Fortunately, artist's brushes are organized in a 1-through-12 numbering system that is used by all the brush manufacturers. You can easily choose the right size even when you're buying a brush made by a manufacturer other than those whose equipment we mention.

The bristle brushes we use for the projects in this book are available in either natural or synthetic bristles. We prefer synthetic bristles because they're of a reliable quality and they're

easier to care for than natural bristles. The brushes you can buy for our projects come from Liquitex, Robert Simmons, Inc., M. Grumbacher, and Loew-Cornell.

A scrubber brush has short, coarse bristles in a round head. It's used to scrub paint directly onto fabric. You may see these brushes called "round" or "flat"; what you want is a brush with a short, coarse bristle. This brush is essential for painting on coarse or heavy fabric such as that of sweatshirts.

A shader has short bristles in a flat head and has a chiseled edge that becomes sharper when wet. It's used to give a flat, wide line or, when placed on its edge, to achieve a crisp, clean, fine line of paint.

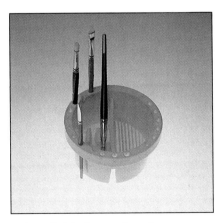

A brush bin keeps brushes neat.

You can clean your brushes in a cup of water. Be sure to choose a sturdy cup that won't become top-heavy when brushes are in it. To use your brushes most effectively, you may want to purchase a brush bin. This is a round plastic tub that's divided inside to separate clean from dirty water. On its bottom, several brush rests keep bristles straight in clean water on one side, while ridges on the other side let you scrape paint off the brush and into the dirty water. The rim of the bin has holes in which to store your brushes. The lid offers a flat area that makes a good palette.

PENS AND PENCILS: Want to sign your work? You can use the fabric pens made by Marvy or Niji, which give an extremely fine line, to write an unobtrusive but permanent signature.

Washable or "disappearing" pens are the type to use when you want what you've drawn to disappear—for example, when you outline a pattern on a garment or show yourself exactly where to place paint for a seemingly random design. Be aware, however, that a pen labeled "washable" actually may contain permanent ink that will remain visible even after washing. So if you want "disappearing" ink, be sure the pen says just that.

Pastel pencils, which you'll find in art supply stores, offer the easiest way to transfer a pattern to fabric. They give a chalklike line that can be rubbed onto a garment, then tapped or brushed gently to disappear when no longer needed. We use Conté à Paris pencils, which are made in dozens of colors. For the projects in this book, you'll need only black to trace onto light colors and white to trace onto dark colors.

GLUE: When you use glue to decorate clothing, always be sure to choose fabric glue, which is specially formulated to withstand machine washing. Of the many brands available, we prefer Slomons Stitchless Fabric Glue and Transfer Medium.

CRAFT KNIFE: Occasionally you'll need a small knife with a very sharp edge. We use the X-Acto knife, which offers a safety handle and a pointed, single razor edge.

ADHESIVE WEB: Adhesive web is a substance you can affix to fabric to cause the fabric to adhere to another surface. In this book, we use it for no-sew appliqué. Of the many brands and types available, we prefer Pellon Wonder-Under Transfer Web, which has adhesive web on one side and paper on the other. When you have ironed fabric onto the web side, you simply arrange the fabric where you want it and then remove the paper to apply. Wonder-Under, like every adhesive web product, comes with complete directions on its use. Always follow the manufacturer's instructions.

ADHESIVE SPRAY: Some projects require keeping a stencil on your shirt long enough to trace, then removing it without leaving marks. You can hold a stencil in place with one hand, but it's easier to use a spray adhesive such as

that made by Krylon. Be sure to spray only in a well-ventilated area, outdoors if possible.

SHIRT BOARD: Painting on fabric requires a flat, taut work surface that won't absorb paint. Several manufacturers make shirt boards that are the size of a T-shirt and are waxed on one side to prevent paint soaking through the board and making it stick to your garment. Two good choices are Tee-Board and Band a Board. These are used by simply slipping them into the shirt, waxed side up, then taping sleeves and bottom behind the board with masking tape, as described on page 7.

If you prefer to make your own shirt board, simply cut a large, sturdy rectangle of cardboard to measure about 20 inches wide by 24 inches long. (A child's shirt or an extra-large shirt will, of course, require adjustment.) Cover one side completely with waxed paper, using masking tape to affix the paper securely. (Don't use plastic

wrap; it's too slippery to stay in place.)

You can use the same method when you want to decorate the sleeves, neckline, shoulders, or bottom of a shirt, or even to decorate pants. Simply open the garment and locate the center of the area you wish to decorate. On a shirt's arms, this probably will be along the crease. On pants, if you're decorating along the side of the leg, the center probably will be a side seam. Use this crease or seam as your guide to the center. Measure its width at the widest point, then measure the length you'll need. Cut a piece of cardboard to fit the largest part, then trim to accommodate smaller parts, slipping the cardboard into the garment often to be sure you're working accurately.

When you've trimmed the cardboard to fit the garment, cover the board completely with waxed paper, taping it on securely with masking tape. You're now ready to decorate.

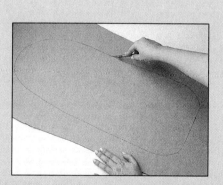  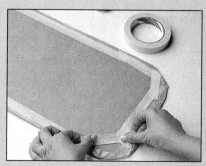

To make a shirt board or a special board for sleeves or pants, cut a piece of cardboard to fit (*above, left*). Check the size by trying your garment on it (*above, right*). Cover one side with waxed paper (*right*).

Choosing, Preparing, and Caring for Your Garments

You can successfully paint many fabrics, including silk, but the techniques described in this book work best on fabrics that are either 100 percent cotton or a blend of 50 percent cotton and 50 percent polyester. A wide variety of styles of T-shirts and sweatshirts are available in those fabrics.

A garment must always be washed before painting to get rid of starches and other residue from the factory, as well as dirt accumulated before you bought the garment. Use regular laundry detergent—not one containing fabric softeners—and dry the garment following the manufacturer's directions.

Subsequent care will depend on what you've used to decorate your garment. The first rule is not to wash a painted garment until at least seven days after painting.

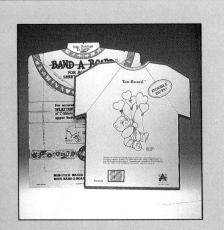

Ready-made shirt boards are a convenient tool for painting on shirts. They are shaped to fit a T-shirt and are waxed on one side.

This is a "curing" period during which the paint sets completely. This period is essential to maintaining the look of your decorated garment.

A cured garment may be washed in a machine set on the gentle or delicate cycle, using a mild, pure soap such as Dreft or Ivory Snow. Regular detergents, including cold-water washing formulations for delicate washables, are not recommended because they contain "lifting" agents. These agents lift the dirt and stains from the garment, and eventually they will also lift its decoration. Fabric softener should be used during the final wash cycle.

A clean garment should be dried by a few minutes' fluffing in a drier set to the "air" setting, then hung to line-dry. (Fabric softener in a sheet may be used during this air-drying period.) Drying with heat can cause your garment to shrink. Worse, it can cause dimensional paint to stick to itself, resulting in peeling and a disappearing design. Even when the garment's manufacturer and the paint manufacturer indicate machine washing and drying are safe, we believe it's safer and smarter to follow these guidelines.

Thinking About Decorating

Much of the fun in decorating comes from learning to be creative with your new skills. Once you've mastered the materials and techniques you'll see in this book, you'll begin to think of other designs, color combinations, and applications. And as you gain the skills to do the work, you'll gain the confidence to try out your ideas.

One easy way to start this process is to take the designs we've shown a step or two further. For example, many of the designs in this book work even better when you continue the design

beyond a strictly front-and-center placement. Consider bringing a bit of the design all the way down to the bottom of a shirt or out onto the shoulders, sleeves, or back. In "Tips and Variations" for projects like this, we tell you how to do it.

In decorating your garments, as in everything involving color, the best colors to use are those you enjoy most. When you'd like to use colors other than the ones we show, choose colors you like to wear and to combine. If you're bewildered by the array of colors available, look at what's in your closet. Which colors do you choose most often? Which are your favorites? If you're decorating for someone else, try to choose colors you can be reasonably sure that person will enjoy—even though they may not be your favorites.

When you're a beginner, it's best to keep color combinations simple, keeping in mind that color combinations work best in threes, fives, or other odd numbers. As you experiment with various fabrics, paints, and techniques, you'll learn what works best for you.

When you design garment decoration for yourself, you're free to emphasize your figure's best points and minimize its flaws. For example, bringing a pattern up onto the shoulders or around the neckline draws the eye away from the hips. And decorating a complete outfit—leggings with a matching T-shirt or sweatshirt, for example—lengthens the body for a slenderizing illusion of greater height.

Consider decorating your clothes an improvisational and spontaneous art. As you work, what looks like a mistake will often turn out to enhance your original plan. Or you can modify your plan to take into account what you've done. Keep an open mind, and above all, remember to enjoy the work.

Harlequin

This striking design blends romantic shadings of soft color with the sharp definition of a white-banded grid pattern. Its use of subtle gradations of color give Harlequin an intricate, complex look—yet this is one of the easiest projects in this book, perfect for the beginner.

Just one technique is needed for Harlequin—dry brushing, which simply means using a dampened brush to thin and spread strips of paint. As the paint is moved across the fabric, its intensity of color fades to the barest hint of tint that shows in the center of each diamond.

The texture that distinguishes Harlequin, giving it a special sparkle, comes from dimensional paint with added coarse-cut crystals of glitter for a shiny, light-catching surface to accent the soft shades of color. The brush for this project is a basic shader, whose flat, soft bristles are effective in spreading the paint to give the soft, gradual fading that's essential to the look of Harlequin.

A rule you'll see repeated at the beginning of every project in this book: Read the instructions at least twice before starting to work.

1. Prepare your shirt by washing, drying, and taping to a shirt board. Place a line of masking tape diagonally across the shirt, corner-to-corner (shoulder-to-bottom). Measure evenly spaced parallel lines to form a row across the shirt, placing lines 2 to 2½ inches apart. Place tape along the lines as you go, making sure all edges are down securely.

2. When all diagonal lines in one direction have been set, repeat measuring and taping starting from the opposite shoulder-to-bottom line. Continue taping until a grid pattern of diamond shapes covers the shirt.

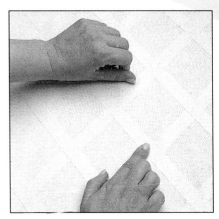

3. When all the lines in both directions have been set, lift the shirt to your eye level and closely examine all the edges of tape. Be sure they are flat and secure to prevent paint from leaking under the tape.

What You'll Need

- **White jersey shirt: we used one of all cotton**

- **Ruler**

- **¾-inch masking tape**

- **Permanent marker: we used a Sanford Sharpie extra fine permanent marker**

- **Shader brush: we used Tulip by Marx Medium Flat**

- **Crystal dimensional paint in three colors: we used Crystal Gala Color in orchid, snowflake white, and peacock**

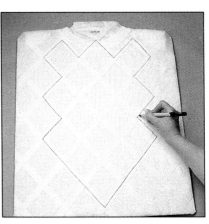

4. Decide on the area you wish to decorate with paint and outline it, using permanent marker to indicate the outline on the masking tape.

5. First, paint the top row of diamonds. Dampen the brush. Blot it to remove excess water, being sure to dry the handle and ferrule. Working directly from the tube, place a line of peacock paint along the taped edge of one diamond, being careful to keep paint on the tape.

6. Using the flat tip of your brush, brush paint from the tape toward the center of the diamond, lifting the brush as paint nears the center of the diamond to leave a gently shaded edge. Be careful not to paint completely through the center. Repeat Steps 5 and 6 for each diamond in that row.

7. Place a line of snowflake paint along the tape line that forms the side of the diamond parallel to the side you have just painted. Brush this paint toward the center of the diamond, lifting the brush to leave a shaded area near the center of the diamond. Repeat for each diamond in that row.

8. For the second row of diamonds, repeat Steps 5, 6, and 7, using orchid paint in place of peacock.

9. For the third row of diamonds, place a line of snowflake paint on two parallel sides of each diamond. Brush both lines of paint toward the center. Repeat these three rows once, then use peacock and snowflake on the bottom diamond.

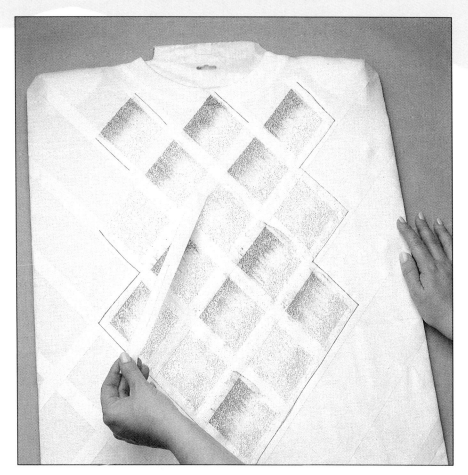

10. Starting with the row of tape you laid down last, gently lift the tape from the shirt. Don't wait until the paint has dried completely, because this may cause the tape to stick to the shirt. Continue removing rows of tape until all tape has been removed. Set the shirt aside to dry.

Tips and Variations

Pay attention to the direction in which you work. Always be careful not to rest your arm on wet paint or smear it as you work.

Although you may wear your shirt as soon as the paint is dry, don't wash it for a week. This is a "curing" period during which the paint sets in the fabric.

Consider extending the Harlequin design onto the shoulder of your shirt and to the very bottom of the shirt. You can use your shirt board to work on the bottom area of the shirt simply by rearranging the shirt and taping it again. To make a shoulder board on which you can paint the shoulder area, see page 10.

Fun with Geometry

If you're looking for a chance to get crazy with fabric paint, here it is! This project exists not only to encourage your zaniest creative whimsy, but to serve as a practice shirt for some very basic painting techniques—working both with a brush and straight from the tube. And if the effect looks complicated, that's because it places paint upon paint for an almost three-dimensional effect.

When we say Fun with Geometry is a practice shirt, we mean it's a very forgiving design. If you try something you don't like, just paint over it. Once you've read through the directions a couple of times, you may decide to try painting on an old shirt before working on your design. That's fine, but don't try to perfect your technique in advance. Much of the fun in mastering fabric painting comes from working out what you wish you hadn't done.

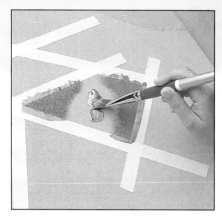

1. Prepare your shirt by washing, drying, and taping to a shirt board. Place strips of masking tape on the front of the shirt in a random-looking arrangement that creates five closed spaces in any geometric shape. Aim for a random look while making sure that the spaces are distributed around the shirt. Each space should contain at least four inches of interior space and be far enough from other spaces so each is clearly delineated. Keep in mind that removing the tape will also remove the lines.

2. For the first shape, place a dollop of each of the three colors of paint within the shape. The dollops of paint should be about the size of a dime. Place one color at one corner, one in the center, and one at the opposite corner. Leave space between them to blend the paint.

3. Dampen the brush, being careful to remove excess water from the bristles, ferrule, and handle. Gently brush the corner colors toward the center of the shape.

What You'll Need

- Sweatshirt: we used one in gold made of 50 percent cotton and 50 percent polyester

- ¾-inch masking tape

- Iridescent fabric paint in at least three colors: we used Delta Shiny Opalescent Fabric Paint in copper, antique bronze, and pewter

- Soft-bristle brush with a relatively large head: we used Liquitex No. 10 nylon flat

- Glitter fabric paint: we used Delta Glitter Stuff for Fabric in gold

4. Brush the center color out toward the other two colors. Shade the three colors into each other with no visible line separating them. Repeat this procedure in a second shape, using only two colors instead of three.

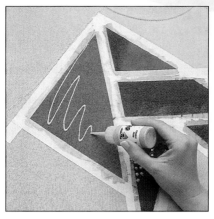

5. Now work with filling in other spaces. Again, place a dollop of paint the size of a dime in one space and brush it out to fill in the space. Repeat this in each space, using one color per space so you'll finish with one copper space, one antique bronze space, and one pewter space. Cover the spaces evenly with paint.

6. Decorate the filled-in pewter area with gold glitter paint. Working directly from the tube, place a row of small dots along the edge of the tape delineating the space. Then place another row underneath, subtracting one dot. Repeat to create a triangle of dots, ending with one dot at the bottom. If you don't like the looks of some of the dots, create a pattern of lines within the dots.

7. In the copper shape, use gold glitter to draw a free-form zigzag line suggesting lightning.

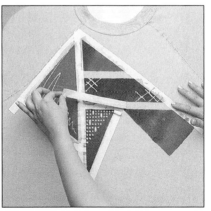

Tips and Variations

Let your imagination go! Think of each geometric shape as a practice area— you needn't worry about ruining the whole shirt if you don't like something you've painted. Just paint over it.

This design is also fun on a T-shirt, but a lighter-weight shirt will support somewhat less paint.

8. In the bronze shape, use gold glitter to draw two grid patterns, one at each end of the shape.

9. When you are finished with all painting, carefully take up the masking tape. Start with the piece put down last and work in that order down to the piece put down first. If desired, draw a large zigzag with gold glitter above the shapes.

Galaxy

Here's the shirt to send a young stargazer into hyperspace! Colorful planets and rockets are arranged on a background of black. Your budding astronaut might want to help by specifying where each planet, comet, and asteroid should go.

This shirt has a lot of detail in it, but the design is surprisingly easy to complete. The whole project should take no more than an afternoon to complete, plus drying time.

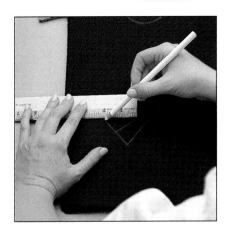

1. Prepare your shirt by washing, drying, and taping to a shirt board. With the pastel pencil, using the bottom of a glass as your guide, outline two circles to form the planets' shapes. To draw a crescent moon, outline a circle and then slide the glass to show a crescent shape. Outline a second curved line to create a crescent. In placing these three shapes, scatter them to leave enough room among them for a rocket ship, shooting star, Saturn's rings, and "stardust."

2. To make the rocket ship, use the pastel pencil and a ruler to draw a triangle with its tip angling upward. Its two long sides should be about 3 inches long and the third side 1 inch long. On the top line of the triangle, draw a fin by extending the short end of the triangle up another inch, then connecting this line to the top of the rocket ship with another 1-inch line.

3. Using paint directly from the tubes, outline each of these shapes in paint, then color in each shape before moving on to the next. We used yellow for the crescent moon, blue for one planet, and stripes of yellow, green, and magenta for the second planet.

What You'll Need

- **Black tank top: we used one made of 50 percent cotton and 50 percent polyester**

- **White pastel pencil: we used Conté à Paris**

- **Round glass in a small size, such as a juice glass**

- **Ruler**

- **Neon fabric paints: we used Tulip Neon Nite Lites paints in yellow, blue, magenta, and green**

- **Glitter fabric paint: we used Tulip Glitter Pen in silver**

- **Wooden pick**

4. Outline the rocket ship in silver glitter paint, then fill it in with paint.

5. Using the silver glitter paint, draw a five-point star, then fill in the star. Draw the star's trail by placing a long arc of glitter at the rear of the star, then gently spreading it outward with your finger. Start at the star end of the arc and spread wider as you move toward the end of the line of glitter.

6. To draw the rocket ship's exhaust, use silver glitter to draw three lines. Place plenty of paint in each line. Gently spread each line with your finger to create a smokelike effect.

7. To place rings around the blue planet, use the yellow paint to draw a circle around the planet, left-to-right. Then use magenta paint to draw a second circle around this yellow ring. Two rings are enough.

8. To make a starburst, place a dot of color on the shirt and encircle it with two other colors. Use a wooden pick to spread these colors from the center dot, dragging the toothpick through all three colors outward in every direction.

9. To complete the background, dot at random with silver glitter. If desired, use other colors sparingly for more dots.

Tips and Variations

When filling in the background as you finish this shirt, arrange some dots in the shapes of real constellations to challenge a young astronomer.

You can add more starbursts, if you like, to bring more color to the design.

Ribbons 'n' Bows

This ultra-feminine design is as flattering as a spray of flowers nestled near your face. It uses a simple, basic painting approach; the secret lies in how you manipulate a spreader to achieve the festive look of a perky bow and the flowing lines of ribbon cascading from it.

When you've read over the step-by-step directions for Ribbons 'n' Bows a couple of times, you may want to practice this technique before starting to work on your garment. As you learn how to move a flat surface to create sweeping lines or a narrow suggestion of curling ribbon, you'll understand the best way to achieve this effect on a shirt.

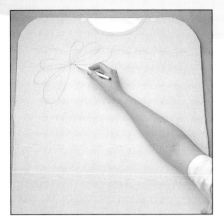

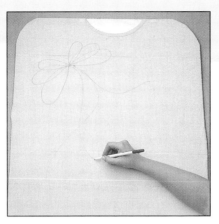

1. Prepare your shirt by washing, drying, and taping to a shirt board. Before starting to work, make sure the cardboard spreaders fit comfortably into your hand. Then use disappearing ink to sketch the bow and ribbon design you want. Mark the center of the bow and sketch in six loops of varying size, placing them in a generally circular arrangement. Avoid a clustered look; try for a natural, almost floppy feeling.

2. Draw in three streamers falling from the bow, aiming for a graceful, flowing effect. Vary the lengths of the three streamers.

3. Place a dollop of the darkest color paint about the size of a half-dollar at the center of the bow. Use one piece of cardboard to draw the paint around the bottom two loops of the bow. Flatten the paint as you go, but be careful not to make a straight, static line. You'll need to work with the spreader to do this, lifting one side or the other and applying varying degrees of pressure. (That's why it's wise to practice before working on your garment.)

What You'll Need

- **T-shirt: we used one in peach made of 50 percent cotton and 50 percent polyester**

- **Disappearing-ink pen**

- **Iridescent fabric paints in at least three colors: we used Delta Shiny Opalescent Fabric Paint in peach, copper, and khaki**

- **Three pieces of heavy cardboard (such as poster board), one for each color you wish to use, each piece measuring about 3 inches by 4 inches; if necessary, trim to fit comfortably into your hand**

- **Glitter fabric paint: we used Delta Glitter Stuff for Fabric in gold**

4. Using the next lighter color, repeat Step 3 on the center two loops of the bow. Use a clean piece of cardboard to spread the paint, trying for a wispy, imprecise effect.

5. Using the lightest color, repeat Step 3 on the top two loops of the bow. With a clean piece of cardboard, draw the paint through the other loops.

6. Now paint the ribbon streamers. Again working from dark colors to light, place a dollop of paint in the center of the bow. Following the lines drawn with disappearing ink, draw this paint down and bringing the cardboard around, up and down for a gently curving effect. Make only one streamer of each color, aiming for a wind-tossed effect as the streamers cross each other.

7. Working straight from the tube, use glitter paint to draw in four more loops in the bow, aiming to accent the bow rather than outlining it.

Tips and Variations

As you work on manipulating the spreader, think of how you decorate a cake with a spatula. That motion—spreading with the flat side, then bringing up an edge—is the basic movement you'll need here.

Consider bringing out the design onto the shoulder and/or sleeve of your shirt. To make a suitable sleeve board, see page 27.

For a complete outfit, decorate jersey pants to match. Place a dollop of the darkest paint at the knee of the pant leg. Draw this paint down in a long, swirling motion to the bottom of the pant leg. Repeat with the other two colors. Add two streamers of glitter as described in Step 8.

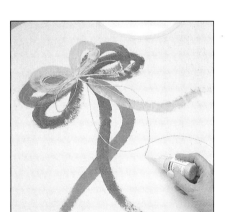

8. Again working straight from the tube, use glitter paint to make two streamers, using a light touch to make very narrow lines with the same suggestion of movement as the painted streamers.

9. Define the center of the bow with glitter paint, drawing a circle about the size of a quarter. Fill in the circle with glitter.

Crayon Mania

From preschoolers to postgraduates, everyone loves the appealingly childlike look of crayons in bright primary colors. If this is your first venture into stenciling, remind yourself that children often create stencil projects. It's easy! Just remember to read the directions completely at least twice before starting to work.

We show this shirt as you'd make it for a youngster, but it's a fun look for kids of any age. Wouldn't a child's care-giver or nursery-school teacher enjoy it as a gift?

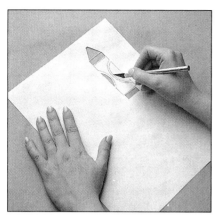

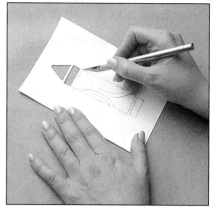

1.   Prepare your shirt by washing, drying, and taping to a shirt board. If you need to make a smaller shirt board for a child's shirt, follow the directions on page 10. Make crayon stencils by tracing the crayon pattern given on page 25 onto paper. Using the craft knife, cut out the areas that appear black in the crayon pattern.

2.   Draw inside the cut-out portion paper pattern to transfer the crayon design onto one of the pieces of cardboard.

3.   Use the craft knife to cut away carefully along the lines. When paint is applied over the stencil, the exposed areas will create a color copy of the crayon pattern in the book. If desired, make four such stencils, one for each color.

What You'll Need

- **White T-shirt with pocket: we used one in white made of 50 percent cotton and 50 percent polyester**

- **Craft knife: we used an X-Acto**

- **Four pieces of cardboard measuring at least 3 by 5 inches (index cards are fine)**

- **Disappearing-ink pen (optional)**

- **Palette: use waxed paper, a paper plate, or the top of a brush bin**

- **Adhesive spray (optional)**

- **Fabric paints in red, yellow, blue, and green: we used Duncan Scribbles Dimensionals**

- **1-inch sponge brush**

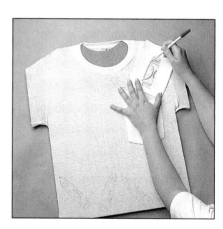

4.   If desired, use disappearing ink to trace exactly where you'll place crayon shapes on the shirt. Aim for a random look, with crayons around the bottom of the shirt and popping out of its pocket.

 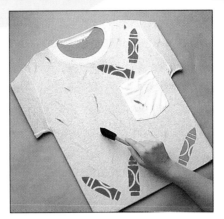 

5. Place a small amount of each color on the palette. Tape the crayon stencil securely on the shirt or spray on adhesive spray. Use the sponge brush to pat color evenly within the open stencil area. Repeat for each color, distributing colors among various areas of the shirt. You may wish to use one stencil for each color to minimize the possibility of color transfer.

6. To create crayonlike streaks of color, dip the pointed edge of the sponge brush into the paint. Use the pointed tip of the brush to gently streak color across the shirt at random, leaving marks no more than 2 inches long.

7. To paint the ribbing and the top of the pocket, dip the pointed edge of the brush into paint. Carefully paint one area at a time, keeping the paint within the seams of each area. Use a different color for each area.

Tips and Variations

It's not necessary to use spray adhesive when you work with stencils, but it does make the job easier. Just be sure to spray in a well-ventilated area. Outdoors is best, but a roomy basement or a room with a fan blowing out of an open window will do, too. In a pinch, use a bathroom with an exhaust fan.

For even more fun with this look, bring the crayons down onto the sleeves of the shirt. It's easy to expand your shirt board to accommodate sleeves. Cut two pieces of extra cardboard, one to slip snugly into each sleeve. Attach these to each side of the board and cover with waxed paper, front and back, making sure no uncovered area remains where paint might seep through. Now place the shirt on the board by slipping the shirt's bottom over the top of the board, stretching gently to get past the sleeve forms without bending them back. Place the sleeves over their board area and secure the shirt area you'll be painting with masking tape. Proceed as described.

Consider personalizing this shirt by stenciling a child's name across the back of the shirt. Cut or buy letter stencils and proceed as for crayon stencils.

Cowhide

Fans of Western wear or the country look will smile at this unusual way to wear their favorite animal! Working on a black shirt may seem like quite a departure, but once you've read through the directions a couple of times, it's a cinch to master the techniques we show you in this project. Cutting a stencil is simple when you use the outline given here, and stamping couldn't be easier. Once you've finished, you can embellish your herd with all sorts of fanciful painted decorations.

What You'll Need

- A large, sturdy black T-shirt: we used one made of 50 percent cotton and 50 percent polyester

- White pastel pencil: we used Conté à Paris

- White fabric dye: we used Delta Starlite Dye

- Textile medium: we used Delta

- 1-inch sponge brush

- **Palette: use waxed paper, a paper plate, or the top of a brush bin**

- **Cardboard, about 3 inches by 6 inches**

- **A new, unused cellulose household sponge**

- **Very sharp scissors**

- **White fabric paint: we used Tulip Iridescent Fabric Paint**

1.   Prepare your shirt by washing, drying, and taping to a shirt board. Using white pastel pencil, trace the area of the yoke that you will paint in a cowhide pattern. From the shoulder seam, bring the line down the sleeve seam to the bottom of the seam. Continue with a randomly curving line across the front of the shirt, then finish at the other shoulder seam. Within this area, use pastel pencil to outline several spots that will remain unpainted.

2.   Thin the fabric dye with textile medium. Place the dye on the palette and, using the sponge brush, paint the yoke area white, leaving the outlined spots black. Allow the painted area to dry at least one hour. In the meantime, make a cow sponge stamp.

3.   Make the sponge stamp by tracing the pattern given at left onto paper or cardboard. Cut out this paper pattern and place on the sponge. Trace around the pattern with permanent ink.

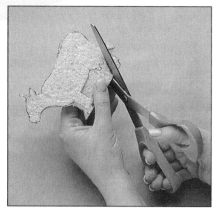

4. Using very sharp scissors, cut away the sponge to leave the cow pattern. This will be used as a stamp. After the shirt is dry, remove it from the shirt board and rearrange it so you can work on the bottom area. Attach it to the shirt board so that the bottom is taut, using the bottom hem as a guide to keeping shirt straight. If you can't fit the entire front of the shirt onto the shirt board, work in two stages.

5. Wet and wring the sponge stamp, leaving it slightly damp. Place more white dye on the palette and use the sponge brush to coat the sponge stamp with dye.

6. Press the sponge stamp onto the shirt, aiming for a mottled effect and stamping no more than twice before recoating the sponge stamp. After stamping cows across the entire width of the shirt, allow it to dry. If you are working in two stages, allow the first part to dry before proceeding.

7. Decorate one of the cows by outlining it in white iridescent paint, using the paint straight from the tube. After a curing period of 24 hours, heat-set in the dryer for 10 minutes at gentle heat.

Tips and Variations

When wringing out your sponge stamp, be sure to wring out all excess water. Drips will thin the fabric dye and alter the look of the shirt.

When you decorate the bottom of this shirt, consider whether it will be worn tucked in. If so, bring the line of cows up so they will remain visible.

Want to "dress up" your cows? Consider painting their udders pink, painting grass at their hooves, awarding one a "blue ribbon" in paint, adding wiggly "moving eyes" or tiny jingle bells to each cow, or writing a "moo" near each cow's mouth.

How about designing your own cow jumping over the moon? Find the nursery rhyme in a child's book and use its illustration to trace cat, dog, spoon, dish, and crescent-moon patterns. Cut each from a sponge and you'll have a charming decoration for your favorite little one.

Leaf Print

As delicate as springtime blossoms or the fleeting shades of fall, Leaf Print is a shirt you'll treasure forever. Choose leaves for their intriguing shapes, or use one from each tree in your own backyard to create a garment with a sentimental secret.

If this is your first venture into printing on fabric, be assured that each step of Leaf Print is easy. It's important to work without rushing, so you can blend colors for their best effect. When you paint leaves, take care to use the underside of each leaf. Painting on its upper side loses the leaf's detailing.

To keep the blended look, you'll find it best to work straight through on this project, finishing before any of the paint dries. As always, even if you're an old hand at this technique, be sure to read through all the instructions at least twice before starting to work.

What You'll Need

- Cotton sheeting shirt: we used an all-cotton shirt in a khaki shade

- Leaves: fresh or silk, in at least three shapes of differing sizes

- Disappearing-ink pen

- Palette: use waxed paper, a paper plate, or the top of a brush bin

- Iridescent paints: we used Tulip Iridescent Fabric Paint in terra cotta, bronze, jade, and khaki

- 1-inch sponge brush

- Glitter fabric paint: we used Tulip Glitter Pens in gold and green

1. Prepare your shirt by washing, drying, and taping to a shirt board. Choose leaves and arrange them on the shirt until you like its overall design; in general, this design works best with leaves arranged in descending order of size. Using disappearing ink, trace each leaf's outline. Remove all leaves.

2. Place dollops of each color of iridescent paint on the palette. Working from top to bottom on one leaf at a time, use the sponge brush to coat the back of a leaf with paint. Coat the leaf completely, but not so thickly that veins no longer show. Make sure paint extends to each tip on the leaf.

3. Place one leaf, painted side down, on the shirt. Press gently to apply paint to the shirt. Be sure to press all the way out to each tip, working gently so as not to tear the leaf. Repeat this process for each leaf. For a blended, fall-like look, don't clean the brush between colors.

4. After painting and pressing all leaves, but without cleaning the brush, place glitter paint on the palette. Put a light coating of paint on the brush and sweep very lightly over one or two sections of each leaf.

5. Using green or gold glitter paint straight from the tube, outline the outer edges of each leaf and highlight its veins and stem. Veins should have a sketchy, broken line. Give stems a light unbroken line.

6. Finish by scattering small dabs of glitter paint on the front of the shirt and between the leaves.

Tips and Variations

Consider a different arrangement on the shirt. This technique produces a

lovely effect as a yoke around the neckline or descending along a sleeve. Also try using

fake gems to highlight several points of your arrangement.

Valentine Doily

Wear your heart on your sleeve—or on your chest—with this charming shirt. Valentine Doily makes the perfect Valentine's Day gift for the sweetest girl you know, and it's sure to be a year-round favorite with anyone who loves the country look.

You might expect Valentine Doily to involve a complicated airbrushing technique, but the delicate shade in its background is easily achieved with paint, water, and any household spray bottle. The shirt's appealing look and simple techniques make it a good project for a child who wants to try working at crafts, especially because acrylic dyes are nontoxic. And it's a perfect chance to reinforce one of the cardinal rules of handicrafts: Before starting to work, always read the directions through at least twice—even if you have to get Mom to read them to you!

What You'll Need

- **T-shirt: we used an all-cotton shirt in white**

- **1 8-inch square paper doily**

- **1 8-inch round paper doily**

- **Spray adhesive (optional)**

- **Palette: use waxed paper, a paper plate, or the top of a brush bin**

- **Matte finish fabric dye: we used Delta Fabric Dye in shadow purple**

- **Any soft-bristle brush with a relatively large head: we used Tulip by Marx Medium Flat**

- **Spray bottle**

- **Fabric glitter: we used Tulip Sparkles in crystal**

- **Fabric glue: we used Slomons Stitchless Fabric Glue**

- **Embellishment: we used Puttin' on the Glitz 4.5-millimeter pearls, 9-millimeter rhinestones, and 4-millimeter amethyst cabochons; you might choose others of similar size**

- **Ribbon: we used 2 feet of ¼-inch double-sided satin**

- **Ribbon rose**

1. Prepare your shirt by washing, drying, and taping to a shirt board. Be sure to remove any bits of paper remaining in the holes of each doily. Arrange the square doily point side up. Cut the round doily in half and place the half-circles on either side of the square doily to form a heart shape. If you wish to use adhesive spray to position the doily on the shirt, spray each piece of doily before painting, being sure to spray in a well-ventilated area. Otherwise, simply hold each piece of doily down as you paint.

2. Place fabric dye on the palette. Working first around the edges and then inside the shape from top to bottom, gently brush paint over the doily just to the edges. Be sure every hole is covered with dye. If the dye seems too thick, thin it very carefully with a drop or two of water. If you thin the dye, be sure to thin it again if you place more dye on the palette so the color is uniform across the entire shirt.

3. Before the fabric dye dries, remove the doily by peeling it off very slowly. The dye will cause some sticking, so work carefully and be sure to get all the paper off the shirt. For the airbrushed effect, place a dab of dye about the size of a dime in a spray bottle. Add 2 ounces of water and shake vigorously to blend completely. Spray onto a white napkin or paper towel to check the intensity of the color. If it's too light, add more dye; if too dark, add more water.

Tips and Variations

You can reuse the heart doily you have made for another shirt; the dried paint makes the doily sturdier.

For a year-round favorite, try this shirt using a round doily instead of a heart shape. Use several doilies of varying sizes and scatter the rounds instead of centering them on the shirt. An easy way to get several sizes is to cut the outer edges from several doilies, making them smaller as you go.

With lots of circles, try using different colors for a completely different look.

To make a complete outfit with either of these looks, run doily shapes down the sides of pants legs.

4. When the paint on the shirt is completely dry—wait at least one hour—place the doily heart over the heart on the shirt to protect it from spray. Spray diluted dye around the edges of the heart shape. Bring the spray out to fade toward the outer edges of the front of the shirt.

5. To embellish, wait until the sprayed paint is completely dry. Place tiny dollops of glitter on desired areas; we used inside straight edges and centers of interior "snowflake" circles. Each doily's pattern differs, however, so you can decide where glitter will work best on your own design.

6. Next, arrange and glue gems as desired, using fabric glue to affix them to the shirt. Place a small amount of glue on the shirt and press the gems into the glue so that glue surrounds the gem.

7. For the top ribbon bow, cut a length of ribbon about 9 inches long. Affix the center to the top of the heart with fabric glue, then loop each side to form a bow. Press these loops down to affix the bow.

8. Glue a ribbon rose to the center of the bow. Repeat to place a bow on the bottom of the heart. After a curing period of 24 hours, heat-set in the dryer for 10 minutes at gentle heat.

Give the Girl a Hand

Here's a concept that invites a million creative variations—most of them based on the idea that more is more, not less! We like tracing adult-size hands to embellish lavishly with nails and jewels. You might prefer more hands that are smaller—those of your children, perhaps? That's the beauty of Give the Girl a Hand—you can have whatever you want.

Remember to read all the instructions completely before starting work on this shirt. The secret to its success lies in taking enough time to plan out the entire design before doing anything permanent. Once you've decided exactly where you'll want every hand and every jewel, putting it all together is fast work. Remember, too, that if you want to decorate the shoulders, sleeves, and back of the shirt, you'll need to let the front dry completely before starting those areas. Allow yourself plenty of time for Give the Girl a Hand and you'll be tickled with the results.

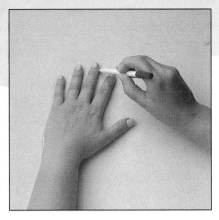

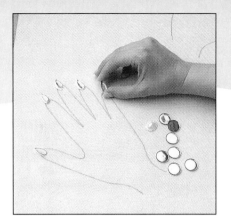

1.   Prepare your shirt by washing, drying, and taping to a shirt board. Using disappearing ink, trace your own hand or the hand you want to use in several places around the shirt. Keep in mind where they'll show up when the shirt is worn—don't embarrass the wearer!

2.   When you've decided where each hand will be, go over the outlines of the hands with pink permanent marker.

3.   Arrange gems on fingernails, ring fingers, and around wrists until you're happy with their appearance. Using fabric glue, affix gems, chain, lace, and other decorations where you want them on the outlined hands to resemble painted fingernails, rings, bracelets, and cuffs.

Tips and Variations

If you want to decorate the back of your shirt, wait until the front paint and glue are completely dry. Then remove the shirt from the shirt board and turn it around to tape the back of the shirt to the wax area of the board. Repeat Steps 1 through 3.

To decorate the shoulders and sleeves, wait until the back paint and glue are completely dry. Make a sleeve or shoulder board following the directions on page 10. After taping the area to be decorated onto the board, repeat Steps 1 through 3 to decorate. Let your imagination go when decorating Give the Girl a Hand. How about painting on a glove or a watch, or using sequins for a bracelet or cuff? You might even copy

a favorite ring or bracelet in fake gems on the shirt.

How about making a shirt using the hand outlines of family members? A shirt featuring the hands and signatures of all the grandchildren would surely delight Grandma. Or try it on T-shirts at a child's birthday party. Each little guest might create a shirt to take home or perhaps simply leave a print—signed, of course—on the birthday child's shirt.

Consider making this a complete outfit by printing palms along the side of a pants leg. A mother might be greatly amused to sport an outfit that looks as if her little ones just wiped their muddy hands on her clean pants!

4.   Use Tulip Sparkles to outline a gem for a ring, creating an opulent setting for the stone. After a curing period of 24 hours, heat-set in the dryer for 10 minutes at gentle heat.

Holiday Packages

Here's a good way to use up scraps of fabric from holiday projects—and make wonderful gifts! We like several fabric patterns for the "packages" on this shirt; using only one pattern could be monotonous. Be sure, though, that each fabric's colors and prints are complementary, not clashing. Put a little time into arranging the packages on your shirt to create a pleasing array before ironing them permanently. Do the same with the ribbons—perhaps bringing them onto the shoulders, sleeves, or back of your shirt.

If you want to create a complete outfit, plan on a few more packages and decorate pants to match. Follow the directions on page 10 to make a board for the pants. Just be sure to read through all the directions a couple of times before going to work.

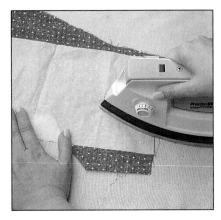

1. Assemble all the fabric scraps you plan to use. Following the manufacturer's directions, iron adhesive web onto all fabric. Cut squares and rectangles from the scraps (we used shapes from three fabrics).

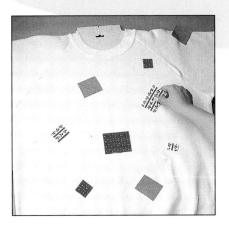

2. Prepare your shirt by washing and drying. Place it over the shirt board, waxed side down. The shirt does not need to be taped. Arrange squares and rectangles on the shirt in an attractive design, moving them around until you like the entire look. Try placing them askew or asymmetrically, keeping in mind that ribbons will complete the picture.

3. When the design is right, peel off the paper backing of the adhesive web. Using a pressing cloth and following the directions given by the manufacturer on the package of adhesive web, iron "packages" onto the shirt on the shirt board. Be careful to seal edges completely. Reverse the shirt on the shirt board so the front is over the waxed side and tape the shirt to the board.

What You'll Need

- **Sweatshirt: we used one in white made of 50 percent cotton and 50 percent polyester**

- **Several ⅛-yard lengths of fabric printed in a holiday motif—not identical, but in complementary colors and patterns; you'll need a total of about ⅜ yard in any width**

- **Adhesive web: we used Pellon Wonder-Under**

- **Disappearing-ink pen**

- **Iridescent fabric paint: we used Tulip Iridescent Fabric Paint in jade**

- **Glitter fabric paint: we used Tulip Glitter Pens in red, green, and gold**

4. To draw loops and curlicues of ribbon beyond each package, first work out a pleasing design by using disappearing ink to draw the ribbons. Begin by bringing the ends of the bows out beyond the edges of each package, working up or down and outward.

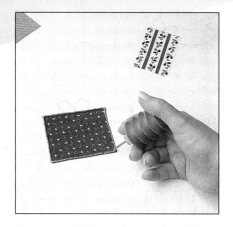

5. Reseal the edges of each package by outlining with iridescent fabric paint, working straight from the tube.

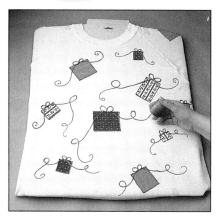

6. Use red and green glitter paint to define the bows, working over the outlines made by disappearing ink.

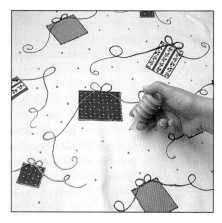

7. Use gold glitter paint to place tiny dots all over the shirt. Make the dots directly from the tube. When you're finished, set the shirt aside to dry.

Tips and Variations

It's crucial to seal edges of packages completely on this shirt. Be generous in painting over ironed edges, and if you notice a spot that's skimpy, be sure to go over it again. This prevents fraying and will keep your shirt looking great for a long time.

Do try bringing the ribbons out onto the shoulder and/or down the sleeve in this design. If you like the idea

of signing your work, try making your signature part of one of the ribbons.

Imagine this shirt in blue and silver fabric patterns for a terrific Hanukkah gift. For a different look, use fabric in children's prints to make a "birthday present" shirt. In addition to ribbons, you might write the birthday child's new age in several spots on the shirt or outfit.

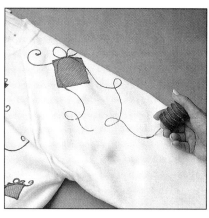

8. To continue the design onto the shoulder of the shirt, wait until the front paint is completely dry. Make a sleeve or shoulder board following the directions on page 10. Then repeat Steps 1 through 7 to decorate.

Victorian Bouquet

Give someone the gorgeous gift of a personal, year-round garden with the rich colors and luxurious blooms of Victorian Bouquet. This shirt uses no-sew appliqué, an easy technique that's endlessly adaptable for other favorite objects— everything from teddy bears to footballs.

Even though this shirt is created with an extremely simple technique, you'll want to read the directions through a couple of times before going to work. This is one project in which it's essential to wash and machine-dry your shirt and the fabric you'll use before starting the work. If either fabric shrinks, the design could be damaged.

Also, pay special attention to choosing the colors you'll use in outlining the patterns on your shirt. They must be complementary, but not precisely the same as the colors in the patterns. You might want to practice the outlining and highlighting techniques described below before working on your shirt. And remember to attach the cut-out pattern pieces securely to the fabric of the shirt.

What You'll Need

- **Cotton sheeting shirt: we used one in black**

- **Preshrunk flowered fabric in a width and length depending on how often its pattern repeats: we used one yard of 45-inch fabric**

- **Small, sharp scissors**

- **Adhesive web: we used Pellon Wonder-Under**

- **Glitter fabric paint: we used Tulip Glitter Pen in multi**

- **Iridescent fabric paint in colors appropriate to your fabric, usually a shade or two darker than the fabric: we used Tulip Iridescent Fabric Paint in mauve and peachfrost**

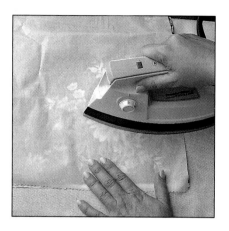

1. Prepare your shirt by washing and drying. Place it over the shirt board, waxed side down. Wash and machine-dry flowered fabric (unless manufacturer's instructions specify otherwise). This step is meant to ensure the fabric will not shrink after being affixed to your shirt. Apply adhesive web to the back of the flowered fabric, working according to manufacturer's directions.

2. Cut out the flowers or bouquet you wish to use, cutting with short, sharp scissors. Arrange pieces on the shirt until you like its overall design. Peel off the paper backing of the adhesive web.

3. Using a pressing cloth and following the manufacturer's directions on the package of adhesive web, iron the flowers onto the shirt on the shirt board. Be careful to seal edges completely. Reverse the shirt on the shirt board so the front is over the waxed side, then tape the shirt to the board.

4. Outline the edges of each fabric piece with glitter paint applied straight from the tube. Cover every edge thoroughly, sealing the edges to the shirt.

5. To accent the flower petals, we used mauve iridescent fabric paint for the darker blossoms. Use the paint straight from the tube to add outlines and accent lines in the flower petals and centers.

6. We used peachfrost paint for the lighter flowers. Use a light touch, following the design, to bring out the dimensional quality of each element.

Tips and Variations

Use a fabric whose background color closely approximates that of your shirt to be sure colors will blend nicely. This also allows you to be less precise in trimming the edges of each cut-out fabric piece.

Do remember to wash and dry shirt and fabric before cutting and ironing. When you're ready to work, think about a free-form arrangement of flowers or about carrying the design out onto the shoulders and/or arms of the shirt.

If you have to cut a specially shaped shirt board to do so, see page 10.

If you wish to add rhinestones, scatter them among and/or between the flowers or bouquets of your design, arranging them until you like the overall look. Affix them to the shirt using fabric glue. Don't forget fabric glue must be heat-set in the dryer for 10 minutes at gentle heat.

Consider highlighting the centers of the flowers with

additional gems or using gems as "dewdrops" on the petals and leaves of the flowers.

This project is not just for Victoriana! Try making a child's shirt with dinosaur or cartoon-character cutouts. Or consider a safari look with animal cutouts, or try a Christmas tree embellished with charms and gems as ornaments.

Conga

Conga is a shirt that says FUN! We like it as a very youthful shirt that, nonetheless, is appropriate for an adult to wear. It's equally appealing for a preteen girl, yet you can achieve a dramatic difference by changing the color of the shirt and ribbons.

To create Conga, gather up every scrap of ribbon you can find—the more the better. It's best to use ribbons that are preshrunk and colorfast—but those should be your only restrictions. We used grosgrain, single-faced satin, double-faced satin, picot, and lace. Once the ribbons were assembled, we found it took a couple of hours to create both of the ribbon fringe pieces.

When you're ready to place the ribbon fringes on your shirt, consider how you want to attach them. To avoid washing the fringes, you can simply fasten them with safety pins, removing the fringes when you wash the shirt. Or you can glue or whipstitch the fringes onto the shirt to skip the step of removing and refastening them.

What You'll Need

- Sweatshirt: we used one in white made of 50 percent cotton and 50 percent polyester
- Ribbon, ¼ inch wide
- 7-inch lengths of white lace, 1½ inches wide: we used 72 pieces
- 7-inch lengths of assorted ribbons in varying widths: we used 216 pieces
- Pinking shears
- Masking tape
- Fabric glue, safety pins, or needle and thread

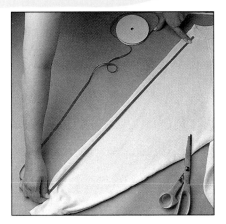

1. Prepare your shirt by washing and drying. Measure one sleeve from the neckline to the top of the cuff. Cut two lengths of ¼-inch ribbon to fit this length. (Ours was 36 inches.) These will be the two foundation ribbons.

2. Assemble a variety of ribbons and laces all cut to 7-inch lengths with pinking shears.

3. To start the first ribbon fringe, tie a length of lace to the foundation ribbon, knotting the middle of the length of lace.

4. Then bring one end of the foundation ribbon up over the lace knot and tie the ribbon to itself so that this knot covers the lace knot. This secures both pieces.

5. Take any length of ribbon and knot it to the foundation ribbon next to the lace. Repeat this step at least twice, then tie on another length of lace. (Our pattern consisted of one piece of lace, three pieces of ribbon, another piece of lace, and so on.)

6. Repeat this sequence until you have filled about 6 inches of the foundation ribbon, then push the tied ribbons close together. Fluff the ribbons to achieve a fuller look. Continue repeating Steps 5 and 6 until the foundation ribbon is full. Be sure to keep knots as close and tight as possible, twisting and fluffing the tied ribbons to achieve a round look.

7. When the ribbon fringe is finished, measure it against the sleeve of your shirt to make sure it is the desired length. Finish off the fringe by knotting the foundation ribbon over the last piece of lace as in Step 4. Repeat Steps 3 through 6 to make the second ribbon fringe, then finish as above.

8. To attach the fringe permanently to the shirt, place a line of fabric glue along the sleeve of the shirt. Press the line of ribbon knots into the glue so that the fringe adheres. After a curing period of 24 hours, heat-set in the dryer for 10 minutes at gentle heat. If you prefer to be able to remove the fringe for washing, arrange it on the sleeve and attach it with safety pins from the inside of the sleeve.

Tips and Variations

Done in black and metallics, Conga is transformed into stunning evening wear—a spectacular top that needs nothing but a simple pair of black pants to become an outfit that goes anywhere.

You can also paint the front of the shirt to coordinate with the ribbons. To spatter-paint, arrange to work in an outdoor area *or other area where it's safe to spatter paint. Thin the paint to the consistency of colored water. Dip a brush into the paint, loading as much paint as the brush will hold. Holding the brush at least 12 inches above the shirt, bring the brush down sharply to fling paint onto the shirt. Set the shirt aside to dry before applying the ribbon fringes.*

Saltwater Taffy

There's a dreamlike quality to the shaded, blended colors of Saltwater Taffy that comes from the unusual technique used to create the shirt. The technique uses a basic property of salt: it draws moisture toward its crystals. That action is what creates the suggestion of motion that permeates the design.

This design lends itself to a very personal interpretation in terms of color. Once you've read the directions through twice, feel free to choose your own favorites and see what happens as they blend.

What You'll Need

- T-shirt: we used one in white made of 50 percent cotton and 50 percent polyester

- Disappearing-ink pen

- Palette: use a heavy paper plate, a styrofoam plate, or a plastic plate

- Water-soluble fabric dye in at least three colors: we used Grumbacher Galaxy fabric dyes in comet blue, neptune green, saturn pink, and moonlite yellow

- Spray bottle filled with water

- Brush with soft bristles and a relatively large head: we used Golden Dove ¾

- Salt: we used a 1-pound box of coarse sea salt

1. Prepare your shirt by washing, drying, and taping to a shirt board. Use disappearing ink to sketch the outer edges of the area you'll paint. We painted across the yoke of a shirt, marking with disappearing ink the bottom edge of that area.

2. Place a dab of two or three colors on the palette and thin each with water to the consistency of watercolor, not much thicker than water. Be careful to keep all colors at a similar consistency. Dampen the shirt by misting with a spray bottle. Working in small sections about 3 inches square and keeping the shirt damp as you work, dab the colors onto the shirt, allowing them to run together. Occasionally dip the brush into extra water and add a bit to the design.

3. When the section is covered with paint, sprinkle with salt, covering the area completely without creating a crustlike thickness. Move on to the next section.

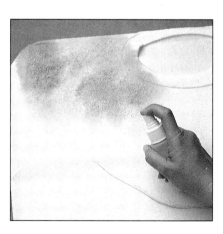

4. Be careful to keep the working area of the shirt wet and always to leave a wet edge toward the next section you'll work on.

 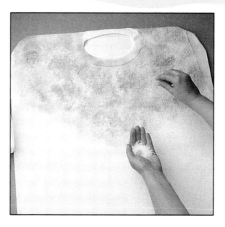 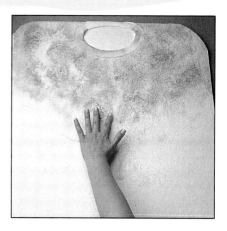

5. Continue working across the yoke of the shirt, repeating Steps 2 and 3. As you work, the colors will begin to spread and run into each other. This gives a pretty, shaded effect.

6. The salt will draw moisture out of the shirt, giving the colors an added dimension. When the yoke is finished, allow the shirt to dry for several hours or until the shirt is completely dry.

7. After the shirt is dry, salt can be brushed off the surface of the shirt with your hand. You can also hand-rinse the salt from the shirt using cool water. After a curing period of 24 hours, heat-set in the dryer for 10 minutes at gentle heat.

Tips and Variations

If paints run together on the plate as you work, switch to a larger plate. Or just wipe away any shade you don't like.

To highlight sections of color, use a touch of dimensional paint or glitter paint. Try using only shades of blue and green for an underwater look, or use bright colors for a psychedelic look.

Remember, this is a free-form project—the results are unpredictable, so get into that spirit and let your imagination flow, too. Saltwater Taffy would produce a beautiful look in a larger area of a garment, even completely covering a long shirt. This is the method to use when you're feeling creative and willing to go with whatever happens!

Mosaic Flowers

Mosaic Flowers introduces an exciting new technique created especially for this book. Like every other project here, the Mosaic Flowers technique is intended for beginners— and this wonderfully subtle, marblelike effect couldn't be easier to achieve. Nevertheless, you might want to practice the technique on an old piece of cotton fabric before working on the shirt you want to keep. Once you've read the directions a couple of times and practiced to master the technique, you'll be surprised and delighted at how easily you can blend colors for a stunning look.

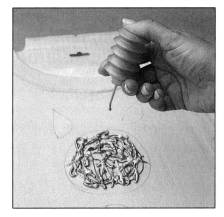

1. Prepare your shirt by washing, drying, and taping to a shirt board. Using disappearing ink, draw circles to indicate where each flower will be on the shirt. Circles should be at least 3 inches in diameter, but keep in mind that paint will spread at least one-half inch beyond the circumference of each circle. Be sure not to place circles too close together. Draw in three leaves for each circle.

2. Working on one circle at a time, place a paper towel under a circle between the shirt and the board. Holding a paint tube about 5 inches above the shirt, drizzle paint randomly inside the circle. Repeat with several other colors, applying enough paint to cover completely the area within the circle. Drizzle with a light touch; the paint will fall in dabs as you work.

3. Drizzle sea mist and liquid pearl paint within the areas you have drawn for the leaves.

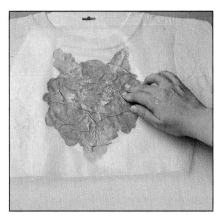

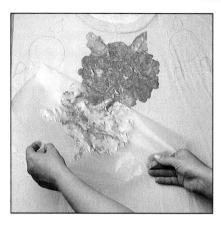

4. Place a piece of waxed paper over the painted area. Working from the center out, gently press with your finger to move the paint outward, smoothing as you go for an even layer of paint and a roughly circular shape. Colors will blend together. After blending flower colors, gently press the paint on each leaf toward the flower and into a generally triangular shape.

5. When colors have blended and you are satisfied with the look of the flower, remove and discard the waxed paper. Place a paper towel, covered with waxed paper to protect your hands, directly on the paint. Press gently to absorb excess paint.

6. Outline the finished flower with blue pearl paint, covering the outer area first. Apply paint directly from the tube, using a light touch. On the inner area of the flower, use the point of the tube to define areas of color in a random fashion. Use loose squiggles of paint, not aiming for precise outlines but for a suggestion of petals.

7. Then outline the leaves using jade paint, adding a center vein and one or two other veins. After outlining, remove the paper towel from underneath the shirt. Repeat Steps 2 through 7 for more flowers.

Tips and Variations

Consider outlining the outer edge of each flower with glitter paint instead of iridescent. (Glitter paint in the inner area of the flower would be too much.) When you've worked with the mosaic technique enough to become skillful, try clustering three small flowers together (remember, patterns work better in odd numbers).

Try the mosaic technique to create a look that's different from the basic flower shown here. For example, you might highlight one area of a garment by applying paint with this technique and manipulating the paint to remain within a certain area. Work toward a mosaic, marblelike effect rather than a flower look.

Yakety Yak!

A teenage or preteen girl would love this playful shirt symbolizing her favorite activity—and so would a grown-up phone freak.

To make Yakety Yak! your own, draw in names and messages that are personal to the wearer. Try bringing the telephone cord up around the shoulder or down along one arm. The basic design is simple, requiring only that you transfer the pattern we provide and paint in the telephone. The rest—the fun part—is explained thoroughly here, so be sure to read the directions through a couple of times before getting down to work. And remember: it's all open to improvisation if you're feeling creative.

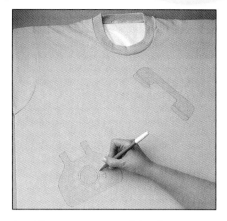

1. Prepare your shirt by washing, drying, and placing on a shirt board without taping the shirt down. To transfer the telephone pattern to the shirt, first photocopy the pattern from the book and cut the receiver from the base, if desired. Place the pieces of the pattern under the shirt so that the pattern shows through the shirt. After you have positioned the pattern pieces exactly where you want them, use a disappearing-ink pen to trace over the pattern onto the fabric.

2. Use the disappearing-ink pen to sketch in the telephone cord and words and phrases to decorate the front of the shirt. When you like the overall design, use the black permanent marker to retrace the words.

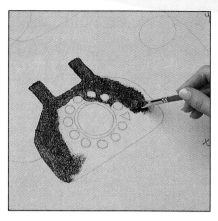

3. Place some of the liquid glitter onto a palette. Re-cover the jar to prevent the paint from drying out. Using the brush, paint in the entire telephone area.

What You'll Need

- **T-shirt: we used one in pink in a blend of 50 percent cotton and 50 percent polyester**
- **Disappearing-ink pen**
- **Permanent fabric marker: we used Niji Stylist II Fabric Marker in black**
- **Black sparkle liquid glitter: we used Tulip Liquid Glitter**
- **Palette: use waxed paper, paper plate, or the top of a brush bin**
- **Brush: we used Tulip by Marx Small Flat**
- **Fabric glue: we used Slomons Stitchless Fabric Glue**
- **Rhinestones: we used 11 Puttin' on the Glitz rhinestones, 11 millimeters**
- **Glitter fabric paint: we used Tulip Glitter Pens in silver and gold**

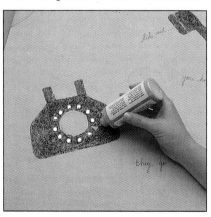

4. Using fabric glue, affix one rhinestone to each "hole" on the telephone dial. Fill in the finger stop with silver glitter paint.

5. Go over the cord line with gold glitter paint, working straight from the tube. Outline the inner circle of the dial, the earpiece, and the mouthpiece with gold glitter. After a curing period of 24 hours, heat-set in the dryer for 10 minutes at gentle heat.

Tips and Variations

Try this design on a white sweatshirt with a red "hot line" telephone. Try dimensional paint to outline the cord or to make the words jump out more.

If you're confident enough, make your own phone pattern for a French phone or even a phone booth. For the French phone, consider using no-sew appliqué to make the telephone a beautiful French country pattern. For the booth, use dimensional paints to color in red and black areas as well as the phone itself. You might even use fabric glue to attach a few quarters to a phone-booth shirt.

Impressionist Garden

The lush, romantic feeling of a French Impressionist painting makes this a very special T-shirt—one you'd be proud to give a very special friend. The sponge brush used to apply the paint gives a softly shaded, blended look that echoes the seemingly random placement of branches. To heighten the shaded effect, we altered the tip of the brush by trimming its edge to a rounded shape.

Note that this project uses acrylic fabric dye, which must be heat-set by machine-drying a few minutes. Before starting to work, take a moment to read through the entire project a couple of times. You may decide to practice splotching on waxed paper or paper towels before working on your shirt.

What You'll Need

- **T-shirt:** we used one in white made of 50 percent cotton and 50 percent polyester

- **Sharp scissors**

- **1-inch sponge brush**

- **Disappearing-ink pen**

- **Acrylic fabric dyes:** we used Grumbacher Galaxy fabric dyes in Neptune green, moonlite yellow, and magenta

- **Palette:** use waxed paper, paper plate, or the top of a brush bin

- **Sparkles:** we used Tulip Sparkles in crystal

- **Glitter fabric paint:** we used Tulip Glitter Pen in multi

1. Prepare your shirt by washing, drying, and taping to a shirt board. Using sharp scissors, trim the tip of the brush to round its top edge and one side. Using the rounded side of the brush will give a smoother curve; the uncut side will give a sharper line.

2. Using disappearing ink, sketch a general pattern onto the shirt. We brought one long branch down diagonally from one shoulder to nearly the bottom of the shirt, making offshoots with several shorter branches in other directions. Place green fabric dye on the palette. Dampen the brush, squeezing out excess water. Dip the brush into the dye; a sponge brush holds plenty of dye, so be careful not to overload. Dab dye onto the shirt, leaving liberal splotches. Fill in along the sketched lines to achieve a full, fern-like effect.

3. Place magenta dye on the palette. Without cleaning the brush, dip it into magenta dye and splotch magenta dye along the branch lines. Cluster these splotches along the branches, but leave green as the most predominant color.

4. Then repeat this process with yellow, clustering yellow splotches with the magenta splotches. This will result in a purplish look. Continue this process, working with each color, until you like the look of the shirt. Don't be afraid to mix colors; this gives the soft, mottled look of an Impressionist work.

5. When you've finished painting, clean the brush. With the clean sponge brush, dab sparkles onto the painted areas, blending them to maintain the mottled look. Dab sparkles over most of the design.

Tips and Variations

For a brighter look, use gold glitter to cover the design instead of the more subtle crystal.

This is a design to bring out your own creativity. Don't be afraid to add more — in working with several colors, exuberance can be just as effective as restraint.

6. Apply glitter paint directly from the tube to sketch on branches. Use short, light strokes to make faint lines, working downward and placing streaks at random. After a curing period of 24 hours, heat-set the dye in the dryer for 10 minutes at gentle heat.

Veronica

A sentimental favorite with us, Veronica is a stunning look that requires some practice and a little patience to achieve. But the sultry Veronica is a seductive beauty, and although this design is more challenging, you might not be able to resist the temptation to make her come alive. When you decide to create your own Veronica, remember to read all the instructions, all the way through, at least twice.

Much of the work on this shirt goes into its earliest stages, which focus on drawing and enhancing Veronica's eye. It's essential to work with care and without rushing through these early steps. When you've finished her face, you'll probably find that creating Veronica's hair goes much more quickly. You'll be glad you made your way carefully to this point when you start swirling those long, long locks onto your shirt. And when you've finished, the compliments you'll receive on your work will be almost as pleasant to hear as they were to anticipate.

What You'll Need

- Sweatshirt in a blend of 50 percent cotton and 50 percent polyester; choose a color you want for the figure's face (white, pink, peach, or beige)

- Permanent-ink fabric marker in black: we used Niji Stylist II permanent-ink marker

- Permanent-ink fabric marker in pink: we used Marvy Fabric Marker Fine Point

- Iridescent fabric paints: we used Tulip Iridescent Fabric Paint in magenta gem (deep pink), turquoise, heather, mauve, and liquid gold

- Palette: use waxed paper, a paper plate, or the top of a brush bin

- Brushes: one No. 8 shader (we used Robert Simmons Tole Master); one nylon flat (we used Dove); one No. 6 round scrubber (we used Robert Simmons Fabric Master)

- Acrylic dye in white: we used Delta Starlite

- Dimensional fabric paint in black: we used Tulip Slick

- Glitter fabric paint in gold: we used Tulip Glitter Pen

- Pastel pencil in black: we used a Conté à Paris

- A gem or navette crystal

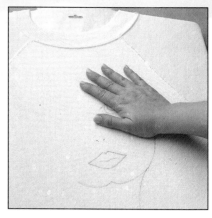

1. Prepare your shirt by washing, drying, and taping to a shirt board. Transfer the pattern from page 64 to the shirt (see page 6 for instructions). When tracing the pattern with permanent ink, use black marker for everything but the lips. Use pink marker for the lips.

2. Place a dab of mauve paint on the palette. Dampen the No. 8 shader brush, removing excess water by wiping from the bristles, ferrule, and handle. Load the brush with paint, stoking paint onto the sides of the brush to heighten the chiseled edge. Carefully place paint inside lips and work out toward their outer edge, bringing paint to the edges with the chiseled edge of the brush.

3. When the mouth is completely painted in, stroke excess paint from the brush onto a paper towel and place a tiny dab of white dye on the palette. (Delta acrylic dye does not need to be thinned with textile medium.) Dip the corner of the brush into the dye and apply it to the inside of the lower lip, blending with the still-wet mauve paint to highlight. Repeat the application of white on the upper lip, again blending well to suggest highlight.

4. Again wipe excess paint from the brush and place a tiny dab of black fabric paint on the palette. Dip the brush in paint and place paint straight across the lips with a gentle downward curve at the center, blending gently into mauve all the way across.

5. To paint the eye, start with eye shadow. Place a tiny dab of turquoise paint on the palette. Use the No. 6 scrubber brush to blend in enough water to achieve the consistency of watercolor, only slightly thicker than water. Load the brush with thinned paint and place the brush in the lower one-third of the eyelid. Then brush outward in each direction, curving downward to follow the contour of eyelid, with the highest point at the center of the eyelid. Do not blend color any higher than the bottom one-third of the eyelid. Because the paint is so thin, it will have a tendency to spread on the shirt.

6. Wash the color from the brush, removing excess water. Thin heather paint as in Step 5. Blend heather in the top of the eyelid, blending outward from the center and being careful to blend heather unobtrusively into turquoise so that no line separates the two colors. Blend heather up to the eyebrow.

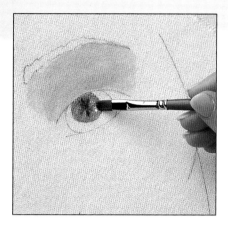  

7. Next, work on the eyeball. Place a dab of turquoise paint on the palette. Using the No. 8 shader, fill in the eyeball with turquoise paint. Without cleaning the brush, pick up black paint from the palette and use it to draw a six-point asterisk in the center of the eye, elongating the bottom line almost to the bottom of the eye. Rinse black paint from the brush and pick up white, highlighting the eye as you did the mouth (see Step 3).

8. To draw eyelashes, load the clean shader brush with black paint. Gently draw over the line forming the top of the eyelid, being careful not to obscure the turquoise eye shadow. Using the chiseled edge of the brush, gently brush up and out to create eyelashes. Lengthen the lashes very gradually as you work, so those at the outer corner of the eye are longest, for a feathery look. Working very delicately, repeat for lower lashes. Allow the eye area to dry a little before proceeding with the eyebrow.

9. To draw the eyebrow, use black paint directly from the tube. Starting from the inside corner of the brow, draw a line of paint tapering gradually toward the outside of the brow. Using the applicator tip, gently brush upward in a few spots at the top of the brow for a feathery effect.

Tips and Variations

To achieve a different effect in Veronica's hair, use only sweeping curves of the brush when painting the hair. This produces a less curly, more wavy look.

For a complete outfit, consider decorating pants to match. Follow the directions on page 10 for making a board to fit the pants. Trace lines in disappearing ink where you want to continue Veronica's hair. Then paint in the hair as described in Steps 10 through 14.

10. Now you're ready to begin Veronica's hair. Place gold paint on the palette and use the flat brush to blend in enough water to achieve the consistency of watercolor, only slightly thicker than water. Use just a little paint on the brush. For the top of the head, create several large loops starting at a point about 1 inch above and to the left of the inner edge of the eyebrow. Use mostly the edge of the brush. Then make several curving strokes downward on each side for long hair, leaving streaks of color rather than clearly delineated lines.

11. Without cleaning the brush, repeat Step 10 using mauve paint. Colors should accent each other without actually blending together. Remember to use strokes to cover the area where the other eye would be. Use the entire surface of the brush to achieve these lines. Use more paint as necessary.

12. Without cleaning the brush, repeat Step 10 using turquoise paint. Apply turquoise over, next to, and near the other colors. Keep in mind that you're creating the shape of the hair—gradually bring the curls out all the way to the sides of the shirt. Bring the curls of hair down the front of the face beyond the chin line.

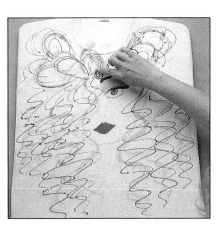

13. Working directly from the tube, finish the hair with just a few squiggles of black paint— only four or five on each side and a few loops among the top loops.

14. Again working directly from the tube, embellish with gold glitter paint to add highlights. Decorate with a navette crystal, affixed with glitter paint.